DIY WINE CORKS

THIRTY-FIVE+

Cute and Clever CORK CRAFTS

Written and illustrated by MELISSA AVERINOS

Adamsmedia
Avon, Massachusetts

Published by
Adams Media, a division of F+W Media, Inc.
57 Littlefield Street, Avon, MA 02322. U.S.A.
www.adamsmedia.com

Contains material adapted and abridged from *The Everything® Guide to Wine* by Peter
Alig, copyright © 2010 by F+W Media, Inc., ISBN 10: 1-4405-0748-1, ISBN 13:
978-1-4405-0748-9.

ISBN 10: 1-4405-7402-2
ISBN 13: 978-1-4405-7402-3
eISBN 10: 1-4405-7403-0
eISBN 13: 978-1-4405-7403-0

Printed in the United States of America.

10 9 8 7 6 5 4 3 2 1

Cover design by Elisabeth Lariviere.
Photos, illustrations, and author photo by Melissa Averinos.

*This book is available at quantity discounts for bulk purchases.
For information, please call 1-800-289-0963.*

DEDICATION

As always, this book is dedicated to my sweetheart, Stuart Schulman. Thank you for believing in me, bringing me coffee every morning, and making my dream of a bright, happy, loving home come true.

CONTENTS

PART 4: ACCESSORIES   79

PART 5: TOYS   113

PART 6: CELEBRATIONS   139

INTRODUCTION

Have you saved cool or meaningful wine corks over the years, either as mementos or in case you ever thought of something to do with them? Well, their time has come. You can use that cork collection to make all sorts of fun projects to display in your home, wear as an accessory, or give as a thoughtful homemade gift. Plus, you're recycling—instead of throwing away your corks, put them to good use. Drinking wine just got even *more* fun!

One of the best parts of crafting with wine corks is that they're so easy to work with. Most of the projects in this book use simple cutting, gluing, and painting techniques with everyday crafting materials. Kids can even join in the fun in Part 5. Plus, it's not hard to find corks—don't worry, you can buy them in bulk if your personal stash runs out.

How to Use This Book

I've divided this book into six parts. The first, "Cork Talk," gives you some background about different types of corks and how to get more of them (besides drinking more wine). You'll also learn about some tools and techniques you'll see later in the book. The other sections—"Entertaining Accents," "Home Décor,"

"Accessories," "Toys," and "Celebrations"—show how you can use your corks for a wide variety of craft projects. Some of these projects call for a little more "crafting" than others—when you're making necklaces, for example. But don't be intimidated—my instructions are jumping-off points, and sometimes "mess-ups" are just happy accidents that create a whole new look!

The most important thing you can do with this book is have fun. So go to it!

PART 1

Cork Talk

Crafting with wine corks is a relatively simple endeavor, but you'll need a little background information before you dive in. In this part, you'll learn about the different types of corks you can find, and how to get more if you need a break from drinking wine! You'll also get a quick run-down of the everyday tools and techniques you'll be using for the crafts in this book.

Corks 101

What *is* cork, anyway? Cork is tree bark! Most cork that you see is bark from the "cork oak," an evergreen oak tree that grows in southwest Europe and northwest Africa. The cork oak's Latin name is *quercus suber*, and if you even make a half-hearted attempt at pronouncing that, you'll notice that the first word sounds kind of cork-y. *Quercus* actually means "oak," though; it's the *suber* part that means "cork."

Cork is a renewable resource, which means when you are crafting with corks, you are crafting green, baby! In fact, the cork oak is not harmed at all by harvesting, which is done by hand with an axe by trained extractors. The bark grows back after nine to twelve years, and can be harvested about twelve times in the life cycle of the tree.

Cork is elastic and nearly impermeable, which is why vintners have used it to seal wine bottles since the mid-1700s.

All Wine Corks Are Not Created Equal

If you drink a lot of wine, you may have encountered several different kinds of corks. The type is chosen by the manufacturer for many different reasons, including quality, price, and how long the wine is aged. Luckily, there are ways to craft with each type! Here is a not-so-scientific guide to the different types of wine corks you may come across:

- **Natural corks:** A solid piece in a chunk.
- **Agglomerated corks:** Granulated cork mixed with a binder and formed; may or may not have solid cork discs glued to the top and bottom.
- **Aglica corks:** A kind of agglomerated cork that is made with a finer part of the cork bark; very uniform and dense. Often has a slight facet, or beveled edge, on the top and bottom.
- **Synthetic corks:** Plastic compounds created to look and "pop" like cork.

The projects in this book use all kinds of corks, even synthetic! Crafting with corks is very forgiving—if you have corks that are in great shape, you can feature them as-is—if not, you can dye, cut, or reshape them! Everyone has her own personal preference. (Personally, I like the irregular texture and variations in color that you find in natural corks.) All that matters is that you like the finished product.

Organizing Your Corks

If you have a large collection of corks, it can be kind of overwhelming to paw through them all to get the corks you want for each project. I suggest you separate them into categories ahead of time so you can easily grab what you need when you're ready to craft.

These are the categories I separate my corks into, and how I like to use them:

- **Natural with cool pictures:** Great to "feature," like in the jewelry projects. I'm protective of these and would not use them to practice a technique on. They are special!

- **Natural with cool text:** Work well in many projects, such as the Cork Board Picture Frame or Retro Sunburst Mirror (for both crafts, see Part 3). I use these more often than those with pictures, but I still save them for special uses.

- **Natural with boring text:** If I look at these and think, "meh," I use them for projects like the wreath or birdhouse, when you need lots of corks but don't want to use your favorites. They're also good for practicing techniques.

- **Natural with printed ends:** Cool to feature in projects that showcase the ends, such as the ring and trivet projects.

- **Agglomerated** (which almost always have boring-looking text, so they don't need to be sorted out within the category): Good for practicing a project with, painting or dyeing, or when you use the cork as just a material, rather than featuring the fact that it's a wine cork (such as in the Heart Decoration, Folk Art Flag, and Peace Decoration, see Part 6).

- **Synthetic:** These work great for the Simple Stamps project (see Part 5)—but otherwise, stick to the natural cork variations.

These are just my preferences. The more you get to know your collection and the different ways to use corks, the more you'll develop your own styles and preferences.

Basic Cork Crafting Techniques

Most of the projects in this book require some simple crafting skills. No need to be intimidated—they are all easy to master. Read on for tips on each technique.

CUTTING AND SANDING

I had the best results using a small woodworker's coping saw. A coping saw is a thin-bladed tool that is shaped like the letter P. You can find one at a hardware store, or online. Use a block of wood under the cork to give you some leverage and height, and go slow.

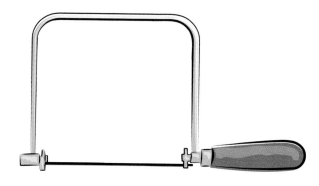

Another way to cut corks is with an X-ACTO knife—a very sharp, razor-like knife that's great for detail work (such as the Simple Stamps project, see Part 5). They're available at craft and office supply stores, hardware stores, and online.

Cutting a cork does leave the edges a bit rough, so I keep two kinds of sandpaper at the ready—rough and fine. The rough grit is useful when you have a very crumbly edge that you need to clean up, while the fine grit works best when you just need to get rid of a few slightly uneven spots. I find it easiest to put the sandpaper on a table and gently swipe the cork across it a few times. A little bit of sanding goes a long way.

Do I Need to Soak My Corks Before Cutting?

I have read on the Internet that you should soak corks in hot water before cutting, to avoid crumbling. But I gotta tell you, I cut hundreds of corks for the projects in this book and I didn't soak any of them. I'd try cutting your corks *without* soaking them first—unless your collection is extremely dry, you probably don't need to bother.

DRILLING

You'll need a drill to make holes for clasps, hooks, and the like. A handheld power drill will do the job. Use the power drill on top of a wood block, to give you some stability and leverage.

If you have and are comfortable using a drill press, you can also use that. Be especially careful when you don't have a flat edge to drill into! The cork can roll around if you don't hold it securely.

GLUING

Since corks are so lightweight, they're relatively easy to glue. When I first started working with corks, I didn't believe that a hot glue gun would make a secure bond. I imagined the corks breaking apart from each other with clumps of dried glue on them. To my surprise, the hot glue worked just great most of the time! Any time the corks are being glued to something for a decoration, the hot glue gun is the way to go. You can find inexpensive glue guns at craft stores and online. Make sure to buy extra glue sticks ahead of time!

You do have a couple of other options, too:

- E6000: This is a very strong crafting glue, available at craft stores. It's a good option if your project is going to get some wear or tugging. Follow package instructions when using.

Always buy more glue sticks than you think you need.

- If you're in a pinch, some carpenter's wood glue or Gorilla Glues will work as well.

DYEING

Dyeing corks enhances them with a nice translucent color, so you can still see the printing and grain of the cork. Readily available dyes like Rit brand work great on corks too. Here are some tips for using Rit:

- Feel free to follow Rit's directions for dye/water ratio—or don't. Once when I didn't have the recommended amount of dye, I found that I still got great results using less dye than they had advised.

- Be careful using dye, because it will stain clothing and nearby surfaces. Wear old clothes, use gloves to protect your hands, and cover surfaces to guard against any splash-over.

- I dye my corks in a plastic shoe container (the kind you buy for organizing stuff). You could also use a bucket or glass bowl.

- It depends on what color you're trying to achieve, but in general, you want to leave corks in the dye for about an hour for a lighter tint or overnight for a deep color.

Rinse until the water is clear. Let them dry on absorbent cloths before crafting with them.

- Experimentation is the name of the game. The color you get depends on how long you leave the corks in the dye; how dark or light the corks themselves are; and whether you're working with real cork, synthetic, or agglomerated. Just try a bunch of different things until you like how it looks, that's all I ever do!

PRIMING AND PAINTING

Painting corks is the way to go if you really want bright color for your project, or to cover writing or images you don't like. And the brighter you want your color, the more you are going to want to prime your corks with a white base. I like to apply KILZ 2 latex primer (available at hardware stores) with a small paintbrush. You could also use a spray primer, artist's gesso, or white acrylic paint as primers. I primed most of the painted projects in this book, but you can do whatever you like. There is no right or wrong, it comes down to preference and time!

For the actual painting, use water-based craft or acrylic paint. I refer to them (interchangeably) as both in the projects, and it really doesn't matter which one you use. "Craft paint" tends to be less expensive, more translucent (requiring more coats), and more matte. Use what you have or what you can afford! Follow the paint manufacturer's directions for application and dry times between coats. Let dry completely before crafting.

Where to Get More Corks

Now that you are ready to get crafting with wine corks, you're wondering, "How can I get my crafty paws on some corks, stat?" Of course, the corks from wine that you drank personally will have more meaning (perfect for the Special Occasion Memento, see Part 6), but sometimes you need more corks than you can harvest after a boozy night with the girls. Here are some suggestions:

- Ask some friends or put out the call on Facebook.
- Check with your favorite restaurants and any local liquor stores who do wine tastings. They get all sorts of odd requests and probably won't bat an eyelash when you ask them to save corks aside for you.
- And the last and inevitable step, once you get into crafting with corks: Order online. There are eBay and Etsy stores that just sell wine corks, or you can buy them in bulk on Amazon. You can get them used, you can get them unused, you can get them blank or printed or all-natural, whatever you want. The Internet is magic.

ASSEMBLING

You'll be using a few types of common crafting closures and tools for some of these projects. They're all readily available at craft stores or online. In each case, I've given you guidance on size and type—but don't feel tied to those suggestions! If I list a ⅜" eye pin and you have a ½" eye pin on hand, go ahead and use it. The parts and tools you need include:

- **Eye pins:** These are pins of varying lengths with a circular end.
- **Jump rings:** These are rings you can use to connect different pieces—chains, charms, etc.
- **Round-nose pliers:** These are useful for bending closures.

Now start making some stuff with corks and drop me a line at *melissa@yummygoods.com* to show me what you made!

Wine Profile: Chardonnay

Chardonnay is undoubtedly the noblest white grape in the world. It can produce the greatest variety of wines in the greatest variety of areas. DNA profiling has concluded that Chardonnay is a cross between the notoriously unstable Pinot Noir and an ancient, and almost extinct, variety called Gouais Blanc. Burgundy claims the title of Chardonnay's birthplace, and there is little to dispute that claim.

Chardonnay is fairly low in varietal character, meaning that it is not terribly impressive on its own, or vastly distinguishable from other white grape varieties. Much of what determines the personality of a Chardonnay is what the winemaker does to the grapes. Using oak to ferment and/or age the wine produces vanilla flavors, while adding richness. Leaving the wine on the spent yeast cells, or lees, adds complexity and a toasty note. Conducting malolactic fermentation reduces the overall acidity and produces a softer, creamier wine. None of this is derived from the grapes themselves.

Chardonnay is hardy and versatile and can grow successfully in all but the most extreme wine regions around the world. It can make great—though somewhat different—wines almost anywhere it's reasonably comfortable. Cool climate Chardonnays tend toward a dry crispness and clean fruit flavors. Warmer climate Chardonnays lean toward richer honey and butterscotch flavors.

In Burgundy, Chardonnay goes into all the region's white wines, such as Montrachet, Meursault, Pouilly-Fuissé, and Chablis. It's one of the three grapes—along with Pinot Noir and Pinot Meunier— allowed in Champagne and the only grape in blanc de blancs. Recently, a series of unoaked Chardonnays have entered the arena and are gaining momentum. Traditionally, famed unoaked styles have come from northern Italy, Chablis, and Burgundy's Mâconnais district.

Chardonnay's versatility is the main reason why it has become one of the most recognized wines in the world. You can expect a tremendous variety of flavors, medium to high acidity, medium to full body, and minimal fruit to tropical fruit. And you can count on a wine that's dry.

PART 2

Entertaining Accents

Of course, corks are right at home in the kitchen or dining room. Since you're already serving wine here, why not accessorize these rooms with fun cork projects? Your guests will marvel at these pieces—from table-top items, like Place Card Holders and Napkin Rings, to cocktail party must-haves, like Wine Glass Markers and a Spreader Set.

PLACE CARD HOLDERS

Meredith

this super customizable place card holder
makes a sweet photo display too

You will need:

* Hot glue gun
* Corks (4 per holder)
* Regular scissors
* Black cardstock (1" × 6" strip per holder)
* Decorative scalloped scissors
* ½" wide glitter tape (6" strip per holder)
* Black florist wire, 1/16" thick (6" per holder)

Why should you be the only one dressed up for a dinner party? Make your table as cute as you are with these easy-to-make Place Card Holders. At home on the dinner table or at a wedding, this project is versatile and fun. You can use them as photo holders around your home when you aren't entertaining.

1. Glue 4 corks together in a cluster, as shown in the photo.

2. With regular scissors, cut the black cardstock into a 1" × 6" strip, then cut with the decorative scissors along the long edges.

3. Cut a 6" length of glitter tape and center over black paper. Press into place.

4. Wrap strip around the cork bundle, overlapping slightly. Trim any excess and glue in place.

5. Cut a 6" length of wire and form into a coil, as shown in the illustration, leaving 2" of wire extending beyond the coil.

6. Gently push the straight end of the wire into the rear cork, as shown in the photo. If it seems unstable, use a drop of glue to secure it.

OPTIONS!

You can mix up the look of this project to your heart's desire. Glitter tape is a great choice when you want sparkle, but you could use other materials you have on hand to create different looks:

* A strip of burlap and some twine for a natural theme
* Striped grosgrain ribbon and an anchor button make it preppy
* Lace and a velvet ribbon lend an air of elegance

coil wire

bend so the loop is centered over the tail

Different Types of Corkscrews

There are hundreds—maybe thousands—of corkscrews available. But they fall into some general categories.

- On the low-tech end of the spectrum are the "**pullers**." They take the form of a T-shape with a handle and a squiggly metal piece (the worm). There are no moving parts, which is why it depends on sheer force (yours) to get the cork out of the bottle.

- The **two-pronged puller** requires less force but more finesse. It has no worm but two blades that you wedge into the bottle to grip the sides of the cork and pull. Professionals like it particularly for older corks that are in danger of crumbling. It's known as the "Ah-So," and it takes some practice to use.

- **Lever-type corkscrews** can take a variety of forms, from something you can put in your pocket to something you can mount on the wall. The most ubiquitous lever type is the butterfly corkscrew. It has a worm and butterfly-winged handles for leverage.

The simplest lever corkscrew is the "waiter's friend"—so-called because it's the favorite among restaurant servers. It's got either a dual or single lever. Then there's the popular "rabbit" corkscrew with gripping handles on the sides and a top lever handle.

Before you can insert any corkscrew into the cork, you have to remove the capsule that surrounds the cork end of the bottle. Cut off the capsule with a small knife or with the foil cutter that comes with many corkscrews. To avoid wine dripping over the edge of the foil, be sure to cut it low enough on the neck of the bottle—under the second lip of the bottle.

NAPKIN RINGS

whip up some of these beaded napkin rings for your next dinner party

you will need:

* Power drill with 1/16" bit
* Corks with interesting prints
* 1mm elastic jewelry cord (about 6" per napkin ring)
* Assorted sparkly beads, size and color of your choice
* Craft glue, if desired

Set a pretty table with some cloth napkins gathered with these sparkly Napkin Rings. You can easily customize this project to match your table linens by varying the beads you use. These would look lovely at a wedding, too—the bridal party could make them together and guests could take them home as a favor!

1. Drill a 1/16" hole in the middle of each cork, as shown in the illustration. Use a toothpick if necessary to push out all of the dust and crumbs from the holes.

drill hole this way

2. Thread corks onto elastic and add beads to cover about 1.5" of elastic on each side.

3. Cut the elastic, leaving a few inches extra on each side.

4. Tie a strong double knot to close the circle. (Don't pull as hard as you can or the elastic will break. It is strong, but don't get crazy!) If it makes you feel better, you can dab a tiny bit of craft glue onto the knot and let it dry. If the holes in the beads are large enough, you can tuck the knot right inside one of them. If not, don't worry about it!

How Are Wine Corks Made?

The techniques used to produce wine corks have changed little over the years. Workers remove the outer layer of bark from the tree and leave it outside for about six months to season. This process allows the wood to dry out. The wood is then boiled to remove contaminants and to increase its flexibility. Next, the wood is cut into strips and the individual corks are punched out of them. The corks are then sanitized, usually with a hydrogen peroxide solution, before being assessed for quality and stored. Only the best cork is used for wine closures; most of it is used for floors and bulletin boards.

TRIVET

don't you love it
when wine companies print
on the ends of the corks?

You will need:

* 37 corks (all the same height and width)
* Hot glue gun
* 1 (22") piece of (⅞"-wide) grosgrain ribbon

This Trivet will protect your countertops—but it looks snazzy enough to use in front of guests on a tabletop, too! This project makes great use of those corks with printed ends. Use them as the center surrounded by corks with plain ends, as shown in the photo, or mix it up however you like.

1. Arrange corks as shown in the photo and glue together.

2. Glue ribbon along the center of the outside of the trivet, making sure to glue and tuck the ribbon into the crevices where the corks meet. Overlap the ends and cut off excess ribbon.

Cooking with Wine

"I cook with wine; sometimes I even add it to the food." It's a funny line from W.C. Fields, but the underlying idea illuminates one of the surest ways to successfully match wine with a meal: Cook with the same wine you serve. There are plenty of wines available for $10 or less that make perfect candidates for cooking, and for sipping while you cook. Trader Joe's is a perfect place to find such wines.

Other great candidates for cooking are fortified wines, such as port, Madeira, Marsala, and Sherry. Each has a massive concentration of flavor, and they have the ability to stay fresh for quite a while after opening, thanks to their high alcohol content.

Wine has certain cooking properties that you should be aware of. Some "rules" are hard and fast because they're based on chemistry. Others are based on common sense.

- When using wine in dishes with milk, cream, eggs, or butter, add the wine first to prevent curdling.
- Add table wines at the beginning of cooking to allow the alcohol to evaporate and produce a subtle taste.
- Add fortified wines at the end of cooking to retain their full-bodied taste.
- To intensify a wine's flavor, reduce it. One cup of wine will reduce to ¼ cup when you cook it uncovered for about ten minutes.
- Using wine in a marinade will tenderize in addition to adding flavor.
- If you use wine in a recipe that doesn't call for wine, use it as part of the recipe's total liquid—not in addition.
- Unless the recipe specifies otherwise, use medium-dry to dry wine.
- Use white wine for light-colored and mildly flavored dishes and reds for darker-colored and more highly flavored dishes.

WINE GLASS MARKERS

this super-quick project
makes an awesome
hostess gift

you will need:

* Coping saw
* 1 cork (makes 4 markers)
* Sandpaper
* Number rubber stamps
* Stamp pad
* 4 eye pins, cut to ½"
* 4 (1") earring hoop findings
* Round-nose pliers
* Optional: Charms with jump rings

OPTIONS!

Fresh out of numeral stamps? Don't fret. You can write in numbers with a permanent marker or improvise with something else. Maybe glue on some acrylic gems, tiny shells, or even some small foreign coins! You could also add a charm before making the closing loops.

Hosting a gathering where people might have some wine? You need to make these drink markers, stat. They are super fast to make, can be customized in so many ways, and are really helpful in making sure guests don't swipe someone else's glass!

1. Use a coping saw to cut cork into ¼" coins. Gently sand.

2. Stamp numbers firmly on cork and let ink dry completely.

3. Insert eye pins into the top of each coin and thread onto the earring hoop.

4. Make a loop on the earring hoop to match the one that is already there, as shown in the illustration.

make a loop on the other end to match

SPREADER SET

the perfect spreaders for your next party

this project really shows off corks with cool prints

you will need:

* Pliers

* Spreader set, the kind where the blade extends all the way into the handle

* Used corks (with corkscrew hole in the center)

* E6000 glue

Pull out this wine cork Spreader Set for use with your cheese platter at your next gathering. This very quick project also makes a thoughtful hostess gift. Look for cheap spreader sets at a dollar store, yard sales, and after-holiday sales.

1.   Using pliers, carefully separate the spreader blade from the handle. Depending on the material that the handle is made from, this may be super simple, or it may require breaking the handle. Once you have the spreader blade separated, discard the handle and clean the blade.

2.   Insert the non-blade end of the spreader into the hole of the cork already made by a corkscrew to dry-fit it.

3.   Remove the blade and put a drop of E6000 glue on the end, and carefully push it in place again. Let dry and repeat for the remaining spreaders. Hand wash with a moist cloth before using on food.

Just say no to ugly spreaders

Wine and Cheese: The Classic Match

Wine and cheese both date back to ancient times—although cheese is the newer kid on the block by about 4,000 years. Wine and cheese both reflect their place of origin and continue to mature as they age. With so much in common, their matchup is a natural.

An old wine merchant's saying goes, "Buy on an apple and sell on cheese." It means that wine sipped with a sweet, acidic fruit will taste thin and metallic. The same wine drunk with cheese will seem fuller and softer. While not all wines pair well with all cheeses, certain pairings are classics:

- Goat cheese and Sancerre
- Brie and unoaked Chardonnay or Pinot Noir
- Mozzarella and Chianti
- Parmigiano-Reggiano and Barolo
- Gouda and Riesling
- Chèvre and Gewürztraminer
- Sharp Cheddar and Cabernet Sauvignon
- Stilton and Port
- Roquefort and Sauternes

With the almost infinite number of wines and cheeses available, experimentation is a fun way to learn. These guidelines help narrow your options:

- The softer the cheese, the more it coats your mouth, requiring higher acidity in the wine.
- The sweeter the cheese, the sweeter the wine should be. Some mild cheeses, especially, have a sweetness that requires an off-dry wine. Dry wines may be perceived as acidic.
- Strong, pungent cheeses need strong wines. Extreme flavors in cheese can be matched by big red wines, sweet wines, and fortified wines.
- The harder the cheese, the higher level of tannins a wine can have.

Wine Profile: Merlot

The 1990s thrust Merlot into the spotlight, as it became the easy-drinking red varietal of choice. In winemaking circles though, Merlot didn't always have star status. It was relegated to the role of blending grape. But its mass-market appeal led to mass plantings around the world. In California alone, Merlot acreage went from 2,000 acres in 1985 to 50,000 in 2003.

Merlot's small, dark blue grapes do not have skins as thick as those of Cabernet Sauvignon, which equates to earlier ripening and softer tannins. The Merlot grape can be traced back to first-century France, but it wasn't named as a distinct variety until the 1800s. While Cabernet gained recognition in Bordeaux's Médoc district, Merlot became prominent in the Right Bank Bordeaux districts of Pomerol and Saint-Emilion. Merlot is the third most planted red grape in France. Besides France, Merlot is important in California, Washington, New York's Long Island district, northeastern Italy, and Chile.

Merlot has a reputation for relatively low acidity and softness. It makes beautiful wines all by itself or blended with others. With its soaring popularity, however, came overproduction in some areas and a tarnished image for many undistinguished wines that were shaped more by market forces than by the winemaker's art.

Most American Merlots do not benefit much from bottle aging. It's a "drink now" wine. Typical descriptions of Merlot flavors are plum, black cherry, spice, blueberry, and chocolate.

CHALKBOARD MENU

awesome for a drink menu . . .

Maple Mark

- bourbon
- ginger beer
- maple syrup
- Lime

. . . or Love notes

you will need:

* 8" × 10" frame with glass
* Sandpaper
* Chalkboard spray paint
* 22 corks
* Hot glue gun

Your signature drink will seem even more sophisticated when you use this crafty menu board to announce it! Chalkboard spray paint and a dollar-store frame (it can even be plastic!) combine to make this fancy-looking—but easy—project. It would make a great gift for those friends of yours who boast a full bar in their house!

1. Remove the glass from the frame and lightly rub one side with very fine sandpaper in a circular motion. Clean it thoroughly with glass cleaner. Make sure there is no lint on it and let it dry.

2. Spray the sanded side of the glass lightly with the chalkboard spray paint according to the manufacturer's directions, and let dry. Repeat several times with light coats until you have good coverage. Let dry completely.

3. To make the corner corks, cut the ends off of 4 wine-stained corks so they're about ¾" tall. Don't worry about exact measurements—the idea is to make them roughly the same height as the corks going around the sides of the frame. Gently sand the edges with the sandpaper and brush off any dust.

4. Glue the corner corks to the frame. Cut the other corks as necessary to make them fit around the frame well. (I used 18 along the edges and 4 wine-stained ends in the corners.) Arrange them all first and then glue into place once you know they will all fit.

5. Replace the glass into the frame with the chalkboard side facing out. Secure the backing behind the glass.

6. Prime the chalkboard surface by rubbing with chalk and wiping with a soft cloth or paper towel. Write in chalk or use those new chalkboard markers—they work great! Display on a table using the pull-out stand on the back of the frame, or hang on a wall with the hook.

OPTIONS!

This project would work well adapted to a larger scale for a full menu. Thrift stores and yard sales are awesome places to find large frames on the cheap. Just use the same steps, but with more corks, and you've got a large hand-made menu board to boast your best brunch. Or, save some money and skip printing individual menus for a wedding— use a large board to announce the meal!

MAGNETS

wine corks + magnets + glue gun = instant gratification

you will need:

* Assorted printed corks
* Coping saw
* Sandpaper
* Hot glue gun
* ¾" round ceramic craft magnets

This is one of those super-easy projects that you can start and finish in just minutes! The most time-consuming part is looking at all of your corks and deciding which prints to feature.

1. Select the prints on the corks that you want to use. The printing can be on any part of the cork. Using the coping saw, cut corks into rounds, sections, or lengthwise halves—whichever method helps feature the printing. Gently sand the back and edges. Wipe off any dust.

2. Glue the magnets to the back of the cork pieces and you're done!

OPTIONS!

If you are looking for something to do with the kids, you could have them paint whole corks with nontoxic craft paint. Let them play with the colors, mixing and painting however they like. When they dry, draw on some simple faces with markers. Glue on some googly eyes and you've got some funny faces for the fridge!

PART 3

Home Décor

The essential function of corks is to close wine bottles, but they are handy in many other ways around the house, too! They make darling Drawer Pulls, and they work great on a Peg Rack to hold jewelry. Cork crafts also make interesting accent pieces that mesh well with a wide variety of home décor styles.

RETRO SUNBURST MIRROR

this statement piece is perfect for above the bar

you will need:

* 9" wooden embroidery hoop
* Power drill with ¹⁄₁₆" bit
* 32 (1¼") wire nails (available at hardware stores)
* 48 corks
* Wire cutters
* 8 round toothpicks
* E6000 glue
* 10" round mirror (found in the candle section of craft stores)
* Nail or small hook for hanging

Reminiscent of those 1950s starburst mirrors, this DIY version adds instant glamour to any room. If you aren't into the natural color of the corks, consider spray painting the corks gold before adding the mirror.

1. Separate the wooden rings of the embroidery hoop and set aside the one with the metal hardware; you will be using the all-wood ring.

2. Drill 32 evenly spaced holes around the hoop, as shown in the illustration. Push the nails through the holes from the inside so the nail head is right against the inside of the hoop and the rest of the nail is pointing out.

3. Push a cork onto each nail. You may need to use something hard to press against the nail head to provide resistance, like the handle of a screwdriver. Make sure the corks and nails are snug and not flopping around.

4. Drill a ¾" deep pilot hole into every other cork on the ring and into an equal number of loose corks. (There should be 16 loose corks total.)

5. Use wire cutters to cut the toothpicks in half at an angle, so both ends of the halves will be sharp.

Mark quarters first.
Then mark 5 spots evenly
spaced between each
quarter for a total of 24.
Drill holes at marks.

6. Insert the halved toothpicks into each pilot hole of the free corks. Insert the other end into the pilot holes in the corks already on the frame. For more stability, you can add a dab of glue between the corks before pressing into position.

7. Hold the mirror over the center of the cork sunburst and take note of how far the cork base extends under it. Turn the mirror over and apply glue where it will have contact with the corks.

8. Carefully place the mirror, glue-side down, on the cork sunburst and firmly press into place. Place a few heavy books on top to create some pressure while the glue dries. Once dry, you can rest the hoop on a nail or small hook to hang it.

PEG RACK

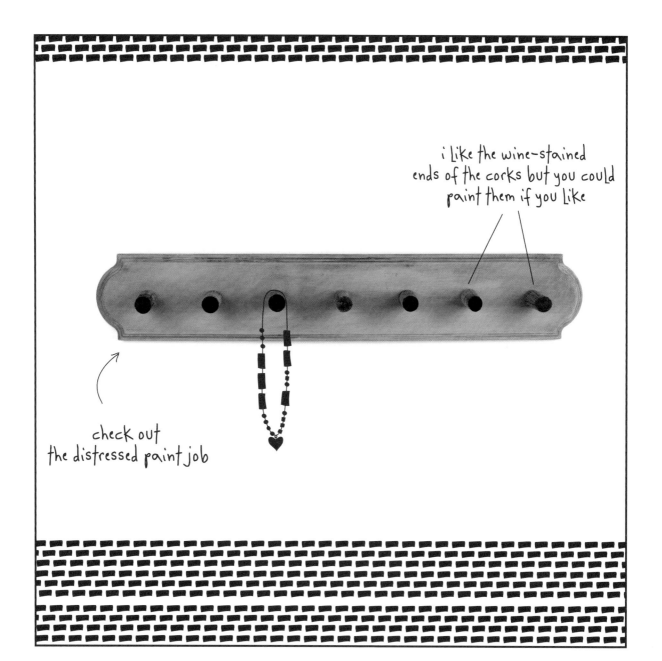

i like the wine-stained ends of the corks but you could paint them if you like

check out
the distressed paint job

You will need:

* Paintbrush
* Turquoise and brown acrylic craft paint
* 23" × 4" unfinished, unprimed wooden board (you can buy these already shaped and grooved at craft and mill stores)
* Paper towels
* Sandpaper
* 7 wine corks, used or new
* Power drill with $\frac{1}{16}$" bit
* 7 flathead screws (1¼" long)
* E6000 or gorilla grip glue
* 2 sawtooth picture hangers
* 2 hooks or nails for hanging

The aged-looking turquoise paint combined with the patina of the old corks give this jewelry display loads of charm. Imagine how pretty all your necklaces will look displayed out in the open instead of stuffed in that box where they get tangled!

1. Use a paintbrush to apply turquoise paint unevenly to the natural unprimed board. Wipe some off with a paper towel and let dry.

2. Mix some brown paint with a few drops of water to thin it out. Paint onto the board and rub some away from the main surface, leaving most of the transparent brown paint in the grooves around the edges of the board. Let dry, then sand in some spots to reveal the wood beneath the paint, enhancing the distressed look. Coarse sandpaper might work best here.

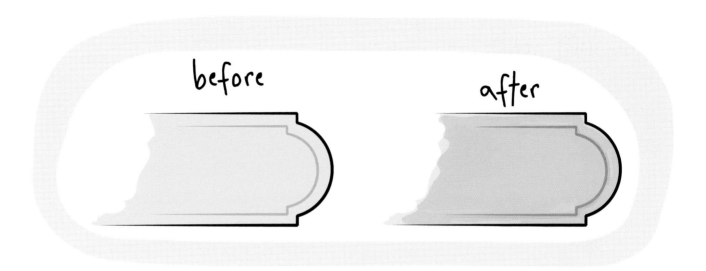

before after

3. Turn over the board to the back and space the corks evenly across it. (The corks will be placed on the other side for the final product; don't worry!) Mark with a pencil where you want them to go, and then drill pilot holes through the board completely. Then insert the screws into the back so they pop out the front.

4. From the front, twist a cork onto each exposed screw, making sure that the base of the cork rests evenly and firmly against the board.

5. Glue the 2 picture hangers to the back, spaced evenly, and hang on 2 hooks.

Top 10 Wine Myths

1. **Aged wine is better than young wine.** Not all wines need aging. Generally speaking, red wines—particularly those high in tannins—require more aging than whites.

2. **Red wine should never be chilled.** Some light reds, like Beaujolais, benefit from chilling.

3. **"Reserve" wines are top of the line.** "Reserve" on American wine labels has no legal meaning. Winemakers can use the term at their whim.

4. **Wines with sulfites will give you a headache.** Sulfites are the cause of headaches in only about 1 percent of the population—mostly asthmatics.

5. **All German wines are sweet.** German wines come in all degrees of sweetness—from dry to very, very sweet. "Trocken" on a German wine label means "dry."

6. **Screw tops are a sign of cheap wine.** Au contraire! Increasingly, top winemakers are using screw tops to avoid cork contamination of their wines.

7. **Wines should always breathe.** In general, breathing is only necessary for wines that need further aging.

8. **All wines have the same amount of alcohol.** The level of alcohol depends on the amount of sugar that has been converted during fermentation.

9. **The more a wine costs, the better it is.** Price is related to many factors: the cost of the vineyard land, the type of grapes used, whether it's aged in oak barrels, and—most of all—the reputation of the winery or winemaker.

10. **Zinfandel is a pink wine.** Zinfandel is a red grape, but it can be made into a red wine or a blush wine.

CORK BOARD
PICTURE FRAME

cool cork board * awesome gift * fun project

you will need:

* 1 inexpensive picture frame

* White primer paint

* Acrylic paint and brush (or spray paint, if you prefer)

* Corks (quantity will depend on the size of your frame, but for reference I used 84 corks in this frame with a 13" × 10" opening)

* Hot glue gun

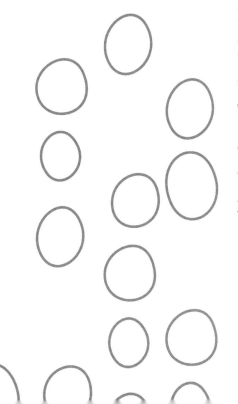

Is this project a bulletin board, or is it a picture frame? It's both! Use it to pin up all your Notes to Self, like you would with a regular bulletin board, or hang one photograph in the center and let the cork act as a mat!

1. Remove the glass and backing from the picture frame. Clean and dry the frame.

2. Prime the frame with white primer paint, and let dry according to manufacturer's directions. Once dry, paint the frame with acrylic or spray paint, as desired. Let dry.

3. Set glass aside (you won't need it for this project) and replace the rest of the backing on the frame.

4. Dry-fit your corks in rows across the entire frame opening. Feel free to cut the length of some of the corks to make them fit. Just take your time and treat it like a puzzle! Glue down corks once the arrangement is set.

DISTRESSED PAINTING

Distress can be a good thing when we're talking about paint techniques! To paint the frame shown in this picture, I used a few different colors of paint in the same general range: orange, fuchsia, neon pink, and dark pink. I didn't fuss too much with it, I wanted it to look haphazard! I just brushed some of each color onto the primed wood, smooshed it around a bit with a brush, added a little more here or there, wiped some off. Then when it was dry, I watered down a little bit of brown paint and wiped it on with a paper towel to give it an aged look. Then I wiped some off. If you like, you could spray or brush yours with an acrylic sealer to give it some shine, but I like how it looks matte. I love the contrast between the wild colors and the aged look!

WHITEWASHED POTS

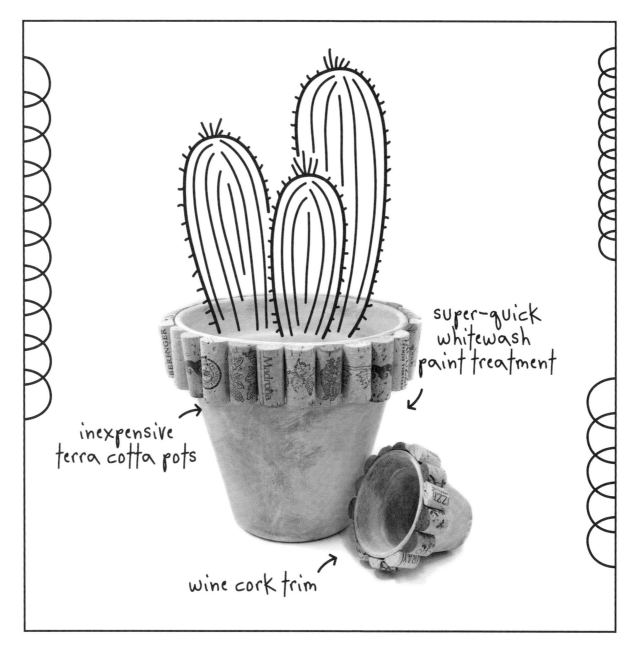

super-quick whitewash paint treatment

inexpensive terra cotta pots

wine cork trim

you will need:

* White paint or white primer paint
* 2 terra cotta pots, 1 (8") pot and 1 (4") pot
* Rag or paper towel
* Sandpaper
* 19 corks
* Coping saw
* Hot glue gun

Whether you use them as planters or catchall containers, these whitewashed terra cotta pots will lend a clean and natural look to your décor. They work best indoors.

1. Whitewash the pots by smearing white paint or primer (whatever you have on hand) on the terra cotta and then wiping it away with a rag. If the paint is going on too thick, water it down a little. The coverage doesn't have to be perfect; you just want a thin and transparent coat of paint on the surface of the pot. If you want the pots to look more distressed, wipe some areas harder with a damp rag so more of the pot shows through. You can also rub with sandpaper once the paint dries to achieve a similar effect.

2. For the larger pot, cut 15 corks cut in half lengthwise with a coping saw. For the smaller pot, cut 4 corks in half lengthwise, and then in half again crosswise. Sand the cut edges lightly and brush off any dust. Glue onto the rims of the pots with hot glue.

OPTIONS!

If you love how the corks look, don't stop at one row! Keep gluing until you've covered the whole pot. Or, spray the pot with chalkboard paint instead of whitewash and write the name of the plant on it with chalk.

terra cotta pots are inexpensive and awesome for crafting

How to Open a Champagne Bottle

Popping the cork is a great way to grab the attention of the entire room, but it wastes bubbles. The cork should be removed so the sound you hear is a soft sigh. Removing the cork in this slow manner also reduces the risks of hurting someone nearby. (After all, there are seventy pounds-per-square inch of pressure in that bottle!) Here's how to safely open your bottle of Champagne:

1. Remove the foil covering.
2. Stand the bottle on a table or counter for support. (It's safer than holding the bottle in your arms and possibly pointing it at someone.)
3. Get a towel. Keep one hand over the top of the cork with the towel between your hand and the cork. Untwist the wire cage. Remove the wire.
4. Keep the towel on top of the cork with one hand and put your other hand on the bottle at a point where you have a good grasp.
5. Turn the bottle—not the cork. You'll feel the cork loosen a bit. Keep a downward pressure on the cork as it completely loosens and finally releases.
6. Hold the cork over the opened bottle for a few seconds to ensure the Champagne doesn't escape.
7. Pour!

DRAWER PULLS

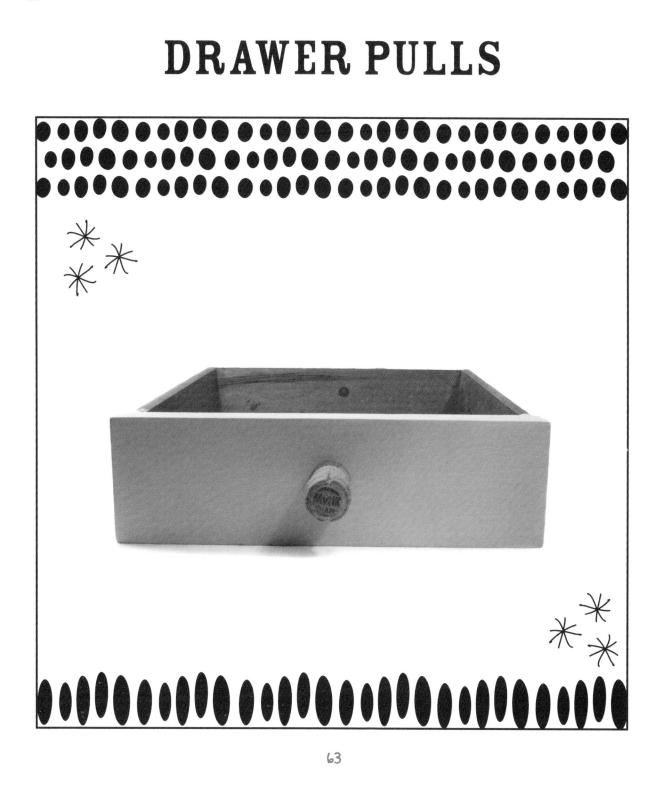

you will need:

* 1 drawer
* Power drill with ³⁄₃₂" bit
* Champagne corks
* ⅛" × 2" flathead screw with washer
* Flathead screwdriver

Dress up your drawers with this superfast DIY. These drawer pulls would be especially awesome on a little sideboard bar! Champagne corks are naturally knob-like, but some of the thicker wine corks would work just as well.

1. Remove existing hardware from drawer.

2. Drill 1" into the cork from the flat end to make a pilot hole. Remove crumbs from hole.

3. Hold the knob against the hole on the front of the drawer. Place the washer on the screw. From the inside, thread the screw through the hole in the drawer and into the cork. Tighten with the screwdriver until secure.

if you only have champagne corks with plain ends, try dressing them up with decorative upholstery tacks

BIRDHOUSE

you will need:

* Paintbrush
* Unfinished wood birdhouse (approximately 6" × 8"; available at craft stores and mill stores)
* Black craft paint
* 20 corks with wine-stained ends for the front of the birdhouse
* Coping saw
* 50–60 printed corks for the rest of the birdhouse
* Sandpaper
* Hot glue gun

This project takes a little while to make, but the resulting *objet d'art* is well worth the time. It would look great perched on a shelf with an abandoned bird's nest and other related items, creating a little vignette.

1. Use a paintbrush to paint the birdhouse black. Let dry.

2. Cut the wine-stained ends off of the 20 corks with a coping saw, making the slice about ¼"–⅜" thick.

3. Cut the 50 printed corks in half lengthwise. This will take some time, so put a movie on and be patient.

4. Sand the cut edges of the corks and brush off the dust.

5. Starting with the sides and then the top, glue the corks to the wood. You can do this any way you like—the photo shown is just an example of how you could do it. You may have some gaps that you can fill in with thin slices of cork if you like. You can leave the back plain or cork it up.

6. Cut one of the remnants of a wine-stained cork at an angle and glue on to the roof as a chimney.

7. Use the wine-stained rounds to decorate the front. I cut a bunch of them in half and used it like trim on a gingerbread house. Get creative with it!

OPTIONS!

* How about a birdhouse with Scrabble tiles spelling out "Welcome" on the front?
* Mix in bottle caps and swizzle sticks for a bar-themed piece to hang next to the liquor cabinet or to give to a boozy friend.
* You could paint the front with chalkboard paint and write your favorite bird-related quote on it.
* You could add a small cardstock banner that says "Happy New Home" and give it as a housewarming present.

Colored Wine Bottles

Why do German wines come in different colored bottles? The color of the tall, slender bottles tells you what region the wine comes from. Brown bottles come from the Rhine region. Green bottles come from the Mosel area or from Alsace. The shape is used elsewhere around the world for wines made from grape varieties associated with Germany—like Riesling and Gewürztraminer.

MIXED MEDIA CAT PORTRAIT

tiny cat art = awesome

you will need:

* 1 champagne cork
* Coping saw
* Sandpaper
* Hot glue gun
* 4" × 4" canvas
* 1 wine cork to cut into ears
* Paintbrush
* White paint or white primer paint
* Acrylic paint
* Paint pens
* Wine corks with letters

The shapes of champagne corks lend themselves to some fun projects, like this tiny kitty portrait. Paint him in the colors of your own pet or make up a furry friend.

1. Cut the champagne cork in half lengthwise with a coping saw. Sand lightly on the cut surface and edges. Brush off any dust and glue to the center of the canvas.

2. Cut 2 (¼"-thick) coins from a wine cork and then slice each of them into ear shapes, as shown in the illustration. Lightly sand them and glue in place above champagne cork.

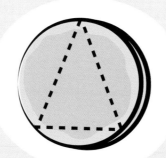

cut triangles for ears

3. Use a paintbrush to prime the cork kitty with white paint and let dry.

4. Give the kitty shape a few coats of paint in the base color of your choice. Paint on a tail.

5. Paint the background, as desired.

6. Draw on the details of the cat with paint pens.

7. Slice up your lettered corks to spell out the name of the cat (or whatever you like!). Glue cork cutouts below the cat.

OPTIONS!

To cut the letters from wine corks, first cut the cork in half lengthwise. Sand the back, and then cut out the individual letters. Sand the sides.

Cutting the words printed on wine corks into individual letters to make words is really fun—and a whole new use for your stash! I bet you can come up with tons of ways to use them. Here are a few to get you started:

* Spell your child's name and turn the letters into magnets for her to practice arranging the letters correctly.
* Spell out a type of wine or short food-related quote on a canvas and hang in the kitchen.
* Make heart-shaped ornaments and glue on "XOXO."

Wine Profile: Pinot Grigio

The French call it Pinot Gris. The Italians call it Pinot Grigio. Americans produce both and drink a ton of it. The Pinot Gris grape exhibits a range of colors from grayish blue to brownish pink. It's in the same family as Pinot Noir and Pinot Blanc but has a character all its own. Pinot Gris (meaning "gray") has been known to produce wines that range from white to light-tinged pink.

Pinot Gris is thought by many to reach its pinnacle in Alsace, where it's called Tokay-Pinot Gris or Tokay d'Alsace. Alsatian Pinot Gris grapes show up in dry, acidic wines or decadent late harvest styles. Just across the border in Germany, Pinot Gris goes by the name Grau Burgunder and produces full-bodied white wines.

That's a far cry from what most people know as Italy's Pinot Grigio—often a light (some might say thin), pale, and herbal wine for easy quaffing. Some of the best Pinot Grigios come from the Friuli region of Italy, where leading producers show full, rounded versions.

The current hot spot for Pinot Gris is Oregon. It was introduced there in 1966 and has become the state's premier white grape. Oregon producers prefer the name Pinot Gris to Pinot Grigio, although there's no single style of wine made. Some winemakers use oak. Others use only stainless steel. Most produce a completely dry wine. Some leave a little residual sugar.

Pinot Grigio has been called the "new Chardonnay" because of its soaring popularity among both casual drinkers and serious wine enthusiasts. Santa Margherita was the first winery to make its mark as an import to the United States in 1979. In the last five years, small growers all over Italy's northeast have been planting Pinot Grigio to take advantage of the demand.

WREATH

you will need:

- 6 (1.5" × 12") strips of muslin
- 12" Styrofoam wreath base
- Hot glue gun
- About 120 wine corks
- Variety of decorative mosses (found in craft stores)
- Feather bird decoration (found in craft stores)
- ⅛" wide ribbon (2 yards)
- 2 (8mm) screw eyes
- Picture hanging wire

Wreaths aren't just for Christmas! The ribbon and pink bird add just the right amount of whimsy to this project. This would make a lovely housewarming gift.

1. Wrap muslin around the wreath and use hot glue to secure. (The muslin has a better surface for the corks to adhere to.)

2. Place the wreath base on a table and glue corks in a row along the inside at the bottom of the base—the smallest circle shown. (The back of this wreath will be flat.) Repeat for the outside bottom of the base (the second-to-largest circle).

3. For the outermost row, glue corks perpendicular to the base, as shown.

4. For the rest of the wreath, return to gluing rows of corks lengthwise until you have covered the whole wreath. You may need to adjust spacing to make sure there are no large gaps.

5. Form a little nest with moss and glue into place. Glue the bird to the center of the nest.

That's right, I put a bird on it.

6. Make little clusters of mosses and glue into place around the wreath. If you did end up with some holes, this is a good time to cover your mistakes!

7. Weave the ⅛" ribbon around the outward-facing corks; tie in the back and trim. Glue in place from the back, if desired.

8. Screw in screw eyes to the 10:00 and 2:00 positions on the wreath back. Secure the picture wire between the screw eyes.

Italy: Wine Powerhouse

Italy produces—and drinks—more wine than any other country. The entire country is practically a vineyard. In 2008 Italy bested France for the title of world's biggest producer for the first time in a decade, at nearly 1.6 billion gallons. Italians consume almost sixteen gallons of wine per capita, an astonishing number when compared to the paltry two gallons per capita consumed by Americans per year. Italy makes more than 2,000 kinds of wine within its borders. Everywhere you go in Italy, you see grapevines growing, and the grapes are overwhelmingly indigenous to Italy, including Nebbiolo, Sangiovese, Barbera, and Dolcetto.

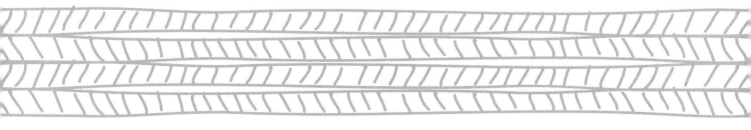

PART 4

Accessories

Introducing corks to your jewelry collection is a great way to save meaningful corks. Wear these versatile items to wine tastings, dress them up for special occasions, or dress them down for everyday use. Don't forget to make some extra for gifts!

WINE AND GEM NECKLACE

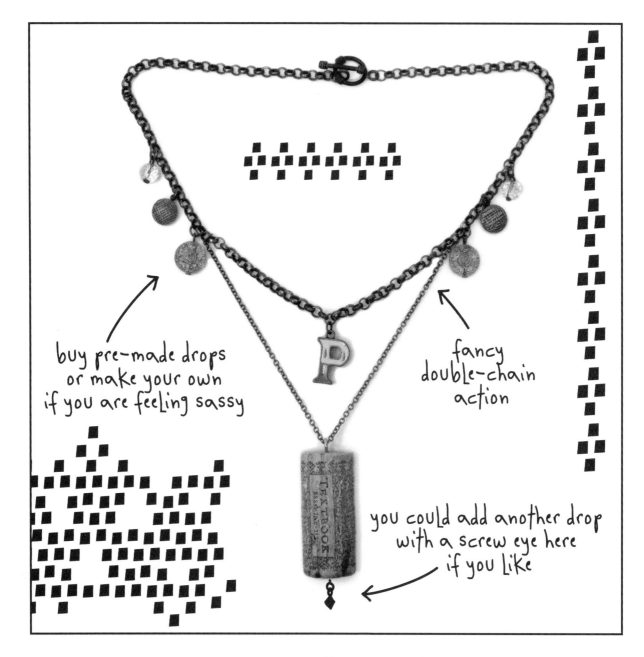

buy pre-made drops
or make your own
if you are feeling sassy

fancy
double-chain
action

you could add another drop
with a screw eye here
if you like

You will need:

* 3 wine corks with red wine stains on the end
* Coping saw
* Sandpaper
* 6 eye pins, cut to ¼" long
* E6000 craft glue
* 7 jump rings (¼")
* 15–20 assorted garnet beads
* 2 (2") eye pins
* Round-nose pliers
* 2 headpins
* Wire cutters
* 12" (or more) chain (I use silver-tone chain and clasps here, but choose whatever you like—or even better, whatever you have on hand!)
* 1 clasp
* 1 jump ring (½")

This elegant necklace uses garnet beads to complement the richness of wine-stained cork ends. Wear this one as a conversation starter the next time you go to a wine tasting!

1. Cut the wine-stained cork ends off with the coping saw, making them ¼" thick. Smooth the back and back edge with fine sandpaper. Brush off any dust.

2. Carefully, but with firm pressure, insert the cut eye pins into opposite ends of each cork disc. Once the hole is made, remove the pin. Squeeze a tiny dab of glue onto the end of the pin and reinsert into the hole you made before. Make sure it is pressed all the way in so you don't have any wire stem remaining, just the eye loop.

3. Connect 2 rounds to each other with small jump rings, then connect the third round the same way.

4. Create a beaded link by threading garnet beads onto a 2" eye pin, leaving about ⅜" unbeaded. Use the pliers to twist the remaining wire into a loop, as shown. Before closing this loop, thread on the top loop of the top cork disc, and close the loop with pliers. Repeat to create and fasten a second beaded link.

5. Make the beaded drops by placing one or two small beads on each headpin and make a loop at the top. If you have extra wire, you can either wrap it around the stem with your pliers or snip it off with wire cutters.

6. Attach one drop to the bottom of the necklace with a jump ring.

7. Cut the 12" of chain into two equal parts.

8. Attach jump rings to one end of each section of chain and hook onto the free eye of the beaded links. Close the jump rings.

9. Open two more jump rings and thread through the open ends of the chain sections. Attach one end of chain to the clasp, and the other end to the large jump ring that the clasp grabs onto. Before closing, slip the second drop onto the small jump ring that attaches to the large jump ring. Make sure they are all securely and smoothly closed.

Beading 101

For this project, I used 2 round, 1 disc, 1 faceted square, and 11 rondelle beads. (Each bead shape has a name.) You can find beads in bulk online, in craft stores, or sometimes in specialty bead stores in your area. Just make sure you have enough for 2 accent "drops" (at the bottom and top of the necklace) and to fill 2 (2") eye pins.

How to Open and Close Jump Rings

To open a jump ring

twist ends away from each other

Gently grasp a jump ring and pull the ends away from each other forward and backward, rather than out to the sides. Close the ring the same way you opened it.

VINTAGE CORK NECKLACE

elegant yet quirky

i love how the wine-stained cork looks with garnet

you will need:

* 18" aged brass jewelry chain
* 1 "feature" charm
* 8 jump rings (¼")
* 1 cool-looking wine cork
* Coping saw
* Sandpaper
* 1 (4mm) screw eye
* 7" aged brass jewelry chain, thinner than the 18" one
* 6 small, flat beads with holes through the center, not at the top (or charm set sold already beaded on headpins)
* 6 (1") headpins
* 1 toggle clasp
* Needle-nose pliers

Natural cork and an aged-looking chain help to create the vintage vibe of this necklace. This is the perfect showcase for one of your favorite printed corks. You could change it up by using charms that relate to the picture on the cork, as in the Key Chain (see project in this part). Get creative and use what you have!

1. Fold the longer chain in half lengthwise to find the center, and use the pliers to attach the "feature" charm to that spot with a jump ring.

2. Cut your wine cork in half lengthwise with a coping saw. Sand the cut back and edges of the cork. Screw in the screw eye and thread onto the fine chain.

3. Hold the fine chain 2.5" to the right and left of the top charm to make sure the charm doesn't hit the cork. If it doesn't, attach the fine chain to the larger chain with jump rings. If it hits, readjust the distance and attach.

4. If you aren't using pre-made beaded drops, make your own by threading the beads onto headpins and closing with a loop. Attach to the large chain with jump rings at the intervals shown.

headpin + bead + loop = beaded drop

5. Attach the clasp to the ends of the main chain with jump rings.

Don't Be Intimidated!

These instructions might seem complicated if you are new to jewelry making, but it's really just twisting a few small metal pieces with pliers. It's harder to explain than it is to actually do, so just trust yourself and dive in. You can totally do this.

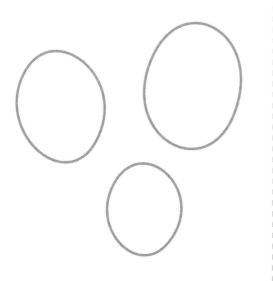

Winemaking in Argentina

Mendoza is Argentina's largest and best wine-producing region. It makes the country's top wines. When Spanish settlers brought *Vitis vinifera* vines to Argentina via Chile and Peru, they discovered that the best place to grow the grapes was at the foot of the Andes. They established the city of Mendoza there in 1561, and it remains the center of Argentina's winemaking industry today. Malbec has emerged as the country's premier grape.

CORK EARRINGS

sparkly, geometric, swirly

you will need:

- 1 cork
- Coping saw
- Sandpaper
- Masking tape
- Acrylic craft paint
- Small paintbrush
- 4 eye pins cut to ¼" length
- E6000 glue
- 2 earring wires
- Round-nose pliers
- 2 faceted beads in a color that coordinates with your chosen paint color
- 2 (2") eye pins

Cork earrings could go so wrong, but with some bright paint, simple wirework, and faceted beads, these babies are a knockout. Experiment with the painted designs and vary the beads to make earrings with different looks.

1. Slice the cork with a coping saw so you have 2 (¼"-thick) rounds. Smooth out the front and back of the cork rounds with fine sandpaper. Brush off any dust.

2. Place one edge of the masking tape directly across the center front of each cork disc. Choose the "front" of the earring based on whether there are fewer cracks on one side compared to the other.

3. Paint the untaped front surface of the cork using a small paintbrush. Make sure not to get any paint on the edges. (If you do, you can just quickly wipe it off with a wet cotton swab, or look at it as a happy accident and paint all of the edges. That is how a lot of my design decisions are made, to be honest!) Let the paint dry and remove the tape.

4. Carefully, but with firm pressure, insert the 4 cut eye pins into opposite ends of each cork disc. Once the hole is made, remove the pin. Put tiny dab of E6000 glue

onto the end of the pin and reinsert into the hole you made before. Make sure it is pressed all the way, so you don't have any wire stem remaining, just the eye loop.

5. Gently pry open the loop on the bottom of the earring wires with pliers by twisting the ends away from each other, rather than pulling them apart to the sides. Thread the top earring loop onto the wire and close it up again with your pliers. Repeat on the other earring.

6. Thread 1 bead onto a 2" eye pin. To create the coil, grasp the plain end of the pin with your round-nose pliers and turn the end onto itself, making a loop, as shown in the illustration. Now grasp the loop flat within the plier jaws and twist the pliers in small increments to wrap the wire around itself, creating a flat coil, until you almost reach the bead. Carefully grasp the coil with the pliers and bend it, as shown, so the coil is centered under the stem. Repeat on other earring.

7. Open the loop of 1 beaded eye pin by twisting it open rather than pulling it, as shown. Attach it to the bottom eye of 1 cork round, and close by twisting the eye in the opposite direction. Repeat on the other earring.

BRACELET

this is the perfect project to showcase
your favorite printed corks

you will need:

* 7–8 corks with cool printing
* Coping saw
* Sandpaper
* Power drill with ⅛" bit
* 12" (1mm) elastic jewelry cord
* 14–20 beads (about ¼" size)
* Craft glue, if desired

Show off some of your favorite corks with this simple jewelry project. This piece is bold, but comfortable due to its light weight.

1. Cut ⅓ of the cork off with a coping saw, lengthwise, as shown in the illustration. It's like you are cutting it in half, but just giving it a little bit more room for the holes to be drilled. Sand cut edges and wipe off any dust.

2. Drill 2 holes in each cork, as shown, making sure to leave enough room at the base so the cork isn't weakened too much by the holes. You don't want any pieces breaking off! Clean out dust and crumbs from the holes after drilling.

cut about ⅓ off of the length

you are going for the look of a half, but with a little more meat to drill into

drill holes here

3. Measure your wrist and decide what length you want the bracelet to be. Cut 2 lengths of cord in your desired length.

4. Insert a piece of elastic cord through one hole in a cork, and another cord in the other hole. Then, thread a bead on the cord. Alternate each cord with beads and corks until you reach the desired length, and then tie a knot in each elastic with a square knot.

5. If desired, you can add a drop of flexible craft glue to each knot and let dry. Jostle the knots so they are tucked inside the hole in one of the corks.

OPTIONS!

✳ If the beige color of natural cork is a bit bland for your taste, try making it with dyed corks. The printing will still show through—just make sure not to leave them in the dye for too long if you're dyeing with a dark color.

✳ Another chic alternative would be to use metallic beads and to paint the ends of the corks in a matching metallic paint.

Wine Profile: Sauvignon Blanc

Sauvignon Blanc is widely cultivated in France and California. The Loire Valley produces wines that are 100 percent Sauvignon Blanc, most notably the crisp, tart examples of Sancerre and Pouilly-Fumé. Dry white Bordeaux wines are usually Sauvignon Blanc blended with Sémillon and aged in oak.

Sauvignon Blanc is also produced in Italy, Australia, South America, and New Zealand. Historians believe that a Frenchman named Louis Mel first brought Sauvignon Blanc cuttings to California in the 1870s. The vines grew so successfully they spread to other parts of California, such as the Napa Valley, where a vintner named Robert Mondavi was beginning to make a name for himself.

Back in the 1960s when Robert Mondavi introduced a dry style of Sauvignon Blanc, he wanted to distinguish it from sweeter, blander versions. He called the new wine Fumé Blanc. Rather than trademark the name for his exclusive use, he permitted other wine-makers to use it. Many American wineries label their Sauvignon Blanc wines Fumé Blanc. The labeling can be confusing, but Sauvignon Blanc and Fumé Blanc are the same wine.

Whatever the particular style, you can recognize a Sauvignon Blanc by its distinctive aromas and flavors. Wines from cooler climates are grassy or herbaceous; from warmer climates they develop citrus and tropical characteristics; and in the late harvest style they take on notes of honey and roasted nuts.

SILK YOYO BROOCH

wear a few of these in different colors and sizes
to add some real pop to a plain blazer

you will need:

* Dupioni silk, 4" round piece
* Needle and thread, doubled and knotted at the end
* Wine cork with cool graphics
* Coping saw
* Sandpaper
* E6000 glue
* 1 (3") piece of (1.5"-wide) grosgrain ribbon
* Regular scissors
* 1 (1¼") pin back

I love mixing textiles with jewelry, and this project is an easy way to do just that. You could experiment with different kinds of fabric and ribbon, or incorporate dyed corks, charms, or beads.

1. Make the yoyo by folding the outside edge of the silk under ¼" and sewing a running stitch close to the edge, as shown in the illustration.

fold the edge of the fabric and stitch loosely

2. Gently gather the fabric by pulling on the thread to close the hole almost all the way. Knot and trim the thread. You want the folded-under edge to be on the inside of the brooch.

3. Cut the cork in half lengthwise with a coping saw, and trim from the sides any unprinted or undesired cork. Sand gently and brush off dust.

4. Smear some glue on the back of the cork and press into place in the center of the yoyo. Let dry.

5. Fold the ribbon lengthwise and cut at an angle, as shown in the illustration. Fold over the uncut end about ½" and sew or glue to center back of the yoyo. (This ensures that ribbon doesn't unravel.)

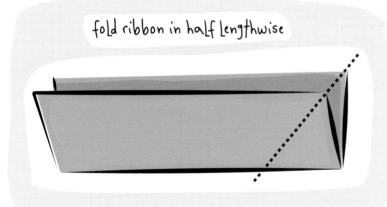

fold ribbon in half lengthwise

snip on the dotted line to make the notch

6. Glue the pin back in place on the back of the yoyo, on top of the folded-over ribbon. Let dry.

Wine-Making in New York

New York is the third largest wine-producing state in the United States after California and Washington, but it often gets overlooked in the mind of the public. Until 1960, New York wines came from native American varieties such as Concord, Catawba, Niagara, and Delaware and hybrid grapes such as Seyval Blanc and Baco Noir. The hybrids, in particular, are still produced, but the more popular *Vitis vinifera* wines have usurped their position. Given New York's rank among wine-producing states, the state is perhaps better known for its grape juice. Welch's grape juice is made from the Concord grape, which flourishes in New York. In fact, about 50 percent of New York's grapes become grape juice.

CHARM PIN

tiny screw eyes + wine corks = magic

You will need:

* 1 cork with interesting printing
* Coping saw
* Sandpaper
* Needle-nose pliers
* 1 main center charm
* 2 smaller charms
* 3 (¼" × ½") screw eyes
* 3 jump rings (¼")
* E6000 glue
* 1 (1¼") pin back

This charming pin is another opportunity to use your corks with the most interesting designs. I love to find images or words that pair well with charms, like this crown cork and bee charm, making a "queen bee" pin.

1. Cut the cork in half lengthwise with a coping saw. Gently sand the cut edges and back. Brush off any remaining dust.

2. Using pliers, attach the charms to screw eyes with the jump rings.

3. Screw the screw eyes with charms, evenly spaced, into the bottom of the cork.

4. Glue on pin back to the back of the cork.

OPTIONS!

✳ Use 3 different charms.
✳ Use smaller charms and use more of them.
✳ Attach a chain to the 2 outside screw eyes instead of charms.
✳ Use the cork lengthwise and use just 1 charm.

try adding chain instead of all charms

Why Is So Much U.S. Wine Produced in California?

California is, hands down, the wine capital of the United States. It accounts for more than 90 percent of all the wines made in the country and 75 percent of all the wines consumed within its borders. The climate has a lot to do with California's preeminence. Not only is it ideal for growing grapes, it is so reliable that there is little variation in the wine from year to year. Getting enough sun every year to ripen the grapes is never a problem in California. The challenge is to find areas cool enough to allow the grapes to ripen slowly, thus allowing full flavor development.

KEY CHAIN

for extra credit select a charm that coordinates with the print on the cork

you will need:

* 1 small jump ring (¼")
* 1 charm
* 1 (⅜") screw eye
* 1 cork with interesting writing or graphics
* 1 split key ring
* 1 (½") screw eye

This unique Key Chain is a snap to make, but it looks really cool. Take your time looking through your wine corks to find the one with the best graphics, and then see if you can find a charm that relates to it somehow. These are easy to personalize for quick but thoughtful gifts.

1. Open the jump ring and thread on the charm. Thread the jump ring through the eye of the smaller screw eye and close the jump ring securely.

Screw eyes are so great for cork projects.

2. Screw the charm section into whichever end of the cork is going to be the "bottom" of the key chain.

3. Garner all of your strength and spread apart the opening of the split key ring. It will take a little bit of effort, but thread it through the hole in the larger screw eye.

4. Screw the screw eye into the center of the top of the cork and you're done!

Be Flexible and Have Fun!

Don't have both specific sizes of screw eyes? Eh, don't worry about it. Use some that are the same size, or larger than what I specified, or smaller. As long as it gets the job done, who cares? What I'm getting at here is that crafting should be fun. I make up projects based on what I have laying around. It's just crafting—relax, improvise, and most of all—have fun with it!

What Are a Wine's Legs?

When you swirl a glass of wine, little streams of wine fall back down the sides of the glass. These are the legs. They have nothing to do with quality. Wines with better legs generally have higher alcohol contents.

CORK RING

I do! (Love wine)

. . . and glitter

. . . and rings.

you will need:

* 1 wine cork with interesting printing on the top
* Coping saw
* Sandpaper
* Mod Podge Dimensional Magic Glue or Judikins Diamond Glaze
* Gold glitter
* E6000 glue
* 1 blank brass or gold-tone ring

Ahh, glitter and wine, two of a girl's best friends and the basis of this statement ring. This is the perfect project to show off that cool printing you sometimes see on the top of wine corks. Make a bunch at once for your Girls' Night Out cohorts!

1. Slice a ¼"–⅜" thick coin from the printed end of the cork with a coping saw. Gently rub fine sandpaper across the cut edge to smooth. Wipe off any dust.

2. To make the interesting image on the cork end raised and glossy, apply Mod Podge Dimensional Magic or something similar like Diamond Glaze according to the manufacturer's instructions. (Acrylic paint sealer or even clear nail polish would work in a pinch!) Let dry.

3. Shake out some glitter onto scrap paper and squeeze out a lentil-sized blob of E6000 onto a different piece of scrap paper. With a pin or something similar, drag some glue along the outer edge of the cork round in a thin even coat.

4. Carefully roll the edge of the cork in the glitter so that it sticks to the glue. Make sure you completely cover all sides, no bald spots! If you missed some, don't

Mod Podge Dimensional Magic adds a thick glass-like coating

worry about it, just dab a little bit more glue on and roll in the glitter again. Let dry. Brush off any loose glitter.

5. Apply a small blob of E6000 on the round pad of the ring base and smear it around so the whole surface has glue on it. Carefully orient the image on the cork so that it faces the way you like and gently press onto the ring base. Let dry.

Wine Profile: Zinfandel

The reputation of the U.S. wine industry is based largely on the ability of European grape varieties to grow well here. Zinfandel became a particular source of pride in the nineteenth and twentieth centuries because it was considered the only indigenous American grape variety to produce wines that Europeans could respect. However, thanks to genetic testing courtesy of the University of California at Davis, Zinfandel was determined to be identical to the Croatian grape Crljenak Kastelanski. No one truly knows how the grape arrived in America, but the reputation of American Zinfandel wines is secure.

Zinfandel would probably not occupy as much California vineyard land as it does today were it not for the success of White Zinfandel in the 1980s. Zinfandel is a red grape, but when it is crushed and the skins are left to soak in its juice for a few hours, the juice turns pink. Quick removal and partial fermentation results in a sweet, pink, fruity wine that has captivated wine drinkers in the United States.

Red Zinfandel is a completely different story. Zinfandel can ripen to high sugar levels, creating high-alcohol wines with a pronounced viscosity and raspberry, peppery aromas and flavors. Growing Zinfandel requires skill as its large grape bunches often do not ripen evenly.

PART 5

Toys

Are your kids tired of crafting with paper and crayons? Break out the corks and let the kids play with them, too! These fun toys and accessories will brighten any rainy day. Kids can customize these in so many ways—each craft will be as unique as them.

SNAKE TOY

you will need:

* Power drill with ³⁄₁₆" bit
* 18 corks (or more if you want a longer snake)
* Coping saw
* Sandpaper
* Paintbrush
* White nontoxic primer paint
* Green nontoxic craft paint
* Paint pens in assorted colors
* Optional: Clear acrylic nontoxic sealer, brush-on or spray
* ³⁄₈" wide ribbon, about 1 yard
* 2 small plastic pony beads

This bright serpent will slither its way into your heart! Let older children color the detail onto the snake with paint pens.

1. Drill holes in all corks lengthwise. Clean out holes if necessary.

2. Use a coping saw to carve the head and tail end of snake, as shown in the illustration. Sand until relatively smooth.

3. Paint all corks with a coat of primer and let dry.

4. Paint all corks the base color of your choice. Repeat with a second coat of base color if necessary.

5. Add details to snake body and face, as shown in the photo, with paint pens.

6. Optional: Spray or paint sealer on all corks. Let dry.

7. Thread corks onto ribbon and use beads and knots to secure the front and back. Cut the ribbon, as shown, to create the snake tongue.

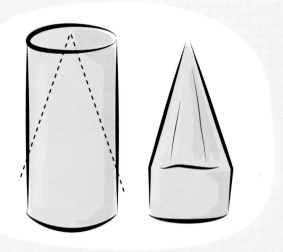

cut the tail cork like you are sharpening a pencil

cut a notch in the head cork like this

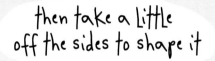

then take a little off the sides to shape it

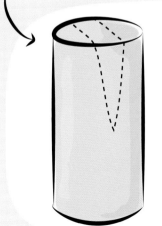

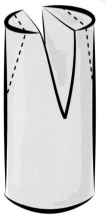

Rosé Wine

Rosé is French for "pink." Rosés are made from red grapes, but the juice and skins are only in contact for a short time (anywhere from a few hours to several days) before the juice is separated. When the winemaker is happy with the color, the winemaking process continues.

SIMPLE STAMPS

finally, a crafty use for synthetic wine corks

you will need:

* Synthetic corks
* Fine-tip permanent marker
* X-ACTO knife
* Stamp pads in assorted colors
* Cardstock

In this case, synthetic corks are actually preferable to real cork because they cut "cleaner" and have a better surface for transferring ink. Take your time with the cutting! Just say "NO" to craft-related injuries!

1. Find the end of the cork that was NOT pierced with a corkscrew—that will be your stamp end. Draw the shape you want to carve with the fine-tip marker.

2. Carefully and gently, slice into the cork at the line you drew, and only take the blade in about ⅛". Then, slice that piece away from the side, as shown in the illustration. (You may want to do a few practice carvings first to get the feel for how the blade cuts the material.) Simply cut away the areas that you don't want to show when you stamp.

3. Test it out by inking and stamping on cardstock to see what the image looks like. Wipe off the ink and make adjustments as necessary until you get the print you want.

OPTIONS!

Make your own stationery with your new stamp set! Buy blank cardstock and envelopes at a craft store, and get stamping. Try printing a border of moons and stars, Xs and Os, or hearts. Or stamp a line of chevrons with a metallic ink pad on black paper—then write your note with a matching metallic paint pen.

FIGURINES

paint pens are perfect for decorating these childhood toy-inspired figurines

you will need:

* E6000 glue
* 1" wooden doll heads from a craft store
* Corks (synthetic will work)
* Paintbrush
* White nontoxic primer paint
* Acrylic nontoxic craft paint, assorted colors
* Fine-tip paint pens in black
* Optional: Clear acrylic nontoxic sealer, brush-on or spray

These adorable little figures remind me of those old-school plastic toys I had as a kid. While these are not for wee ones likely to put things in their mouths, this is a fun project for older kids to do on a rainy afternoon. And, it's another project where you can use those synthetic corks!

1. Apply some E6000 glue to the bottom of the doll head and press onto the end of a cork. Repeat for other figures, and let dry completely.

2. Apply a coat of primer to each figure and let dry.

3. Squeeze some acrylic paint onto scrap paper and brush the background colors of the skin, hair, and clothes onto the figurines. Let dry. Repeat if necessary for more coverage.

4. Add detail with paint pens, as shown in the illustration. Add a tiny dot of white paint on top of the black pupils. Let dry.

5. Optional: Apply 2 coats of protective sealer.

paint the faces like this

or any way you like

OPTIONS!

You can craft these figurines to look like people you know! Just make simple choices based on the subjects. For taller people, use taller corks. Trim corks to make "kids." Paint hair and skin tone to match your subjects, and add little details to their clothes that really reflect the people you are trying to capture in a cork likeness. You could make a set of your whole family, or a couple as a wedding-cake topper!

Grape Skins and Wine Color

The major thing separating red wine from white wine is the presence of the grape skins in the fermentation tank. Red skins add red color to otherwise clear grape juice. It is possible, then, to make white wine from red grapes, although most white wines you buy are made from white grapes. Most white wines come from "white" grapes, which are actually greenish, greenish yellow, golden yellow, or pinkish yellow. Regardless of the actual color of the skins, the juice for white wine is fermented without the skins and seeds. The result is no tannin and little color. White wines can take on a pale straw color or greenish to deep gold tones, depending on the grape variety and aging treatment.

TOY SCHOONER

not just a toy boat, a toy schooner!

you will need:

* Power drill with $\frac{1}{16}$" bit

* 3 corks

* 4 round toothpicks

* Regular scissors

* 1 thin bamboo skewer, at least 9" long

* 1 (12" × 12") piece of printed scrapbook paper

* $\frac{1}{8}$" hole punch

* Washi tape

Add a little twist to the typical cork boat by making it a schooner with paper sails! You could take this in a pirate-y direction by using plain washi tape for the flag and drawing a skull and crossbones on it.

1. Drill ½" deep pilot holes into the corks, as shown in the illustration.

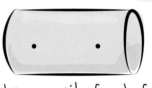

drill pilot holes on one side of each of the two end corks and both sides of the center cork

2. Use toothpicks, as shown, to assemble boat base. (There are two toothpicks poked horizontally through the corks to keep them together.)

insert toothpicks into the holes on the center cork and fit end corks onto toothpicks to assemble the boat base

3. Cut the bamboo skewer into 2 pieces, 5.5" and 3.5". Insert into the first and second cork, as shown.

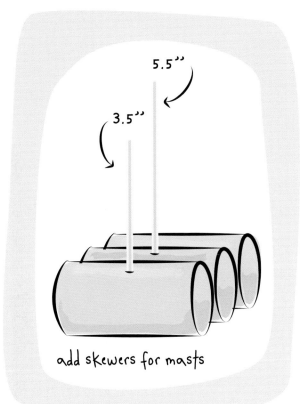

5.5"

3.5"

add skewers for masts

4. Cut 3 sails from scrapbook paper, roughly 2¾" × 2", 2¾" × 2½", and 3½" × 2½". They don't have to be exactly perfect; in fact, it's cuter if they are slightly tapered toward the top.

5. Use the hole punch to make holes in the top and bottom centers of each sail. Thread sails onto skewer masts.

6. Fold washi tape over top of skewers to make flags. Trim if necessary to make edges even.

What Is Washi Tape?

Washi tape is awesome. But what is it? Washi tape is a Japanese craft tape that comes in many colors, patterns, and widths. It's kind of like masking tape, but a little more delicate and a whole lot prettier. I like to use it to decorate envelopes and packages wrapped in brown kraft paper. Start a stash by picking up a couple of rolls at a time. Try layering the different widths and patterns—mix it up and play!

KIDS' NECKLACE

* try dyeing your corks like so

* WARNING : dyeing things can become addictive *

You will need:

* Power drill with ³⁄₁₆" bit
* 7 or 8 corks
* Coping saw
* Sandpaper
* Rit powder dye, assorted colors
* 5 (1") unfinished wood beads
* Optional: Clear acrylic nontoxic sealer, brush-on or spray
* ³⁄₈" ribbon, about 1 yard

This sweet necklace is a great project for kids to help with. Let them choose the ribbon and dye colors, and then they can help with the stringing.

1. Drill holes through the entire length of the corks. Tap out any debris left in the holes.

2. Use a coping saw to cut corks into coins varying in width from about ³⁄₈"–¾". Gently sand cut edges and wipe off any dust.

3. Dye corks and beads different colors according to the instructions in Part 1. Let dry completely.

Dyeing stuff is so fun.

4. Optional: Spray or brush on a couple of coats of acrylic sealer. Let dry completely.

5. String the beads and cork discs onto the ribbon as shown in the photo, or however you prefer. Decide how long you'd like the necklace to be, and make sure this length will fit over the wearer's head with a few inches to spare. Tie a strong knot at the proper length and trim away excess ribbon, leaving ½".

OPTIONS!

This necklace is not just for the little ones, mama! If you made this with a wide velvet ribbon and dyed the cork and wood deeper colors, this would be a statement necklace for you, too. Try adding some sparkly or metallic beads and tie the ribbon in a big flouncy bow for added interest in the back if you wear your hair up.

OWL ZIPPER PULL

dress up your coat with this adorable zipper pull

use a ribbon to transform it into an ornament or gift tag

you will need:

* Coping saw
* 1 champagne cork
* Sandpaper
* Paintbrush
* White nontoxic primer paint
* Regular-tip paint pens in assorted colors
* Fine-tip black paint pens
* 1 zipper pull finding
* 1 (8mm) screw eye

This cute little owl is fast and fun to make. Use my owl drawing or improvise your own! This craft is perfect for party favors at a kids' birthday party.

1. Using a coping saw, cut the champagne cork in half lengthwise and gently sand cut edges and back. Brush off any dust. Save 1 half for another project or a second zipper pull.

2. Paint with white primer and let dry.

3. Use the colored paint pens to color in the owl. If you mess up, don't worry—you can go right over it when it dries.

4. Use the fine black paint pen to create details.

try some Halloween-themed zipper pulls.

5. Screw in the screw eye at the center top of the head, and attach the zipper pull finding.

OPTIONS!

What other things does the champagne cork shape lend itself to? How about a cute red mushroom with white spots? A person? A little fox? Get creative and make up your own! Paint in colors that will complement the wearer's coat.

Wine Profile: Pinot Noir

Pinot Noir has been frustrating winemakers since the ancient Romans. It's recognized worldwide as a premier grape, but it presents obstacles to winemaking every step of the way, from its sensitivity to temperature to its inconsistent propagation.

Pinot Noir first earned its reputation for making the magnificent wines of the Burgundy region of France—and, more specifically, the two-mile-wide stretch called the Côte d'Or. Pinot Noir is also grown in the Champagne region, where it is one of the three grape varieties allowed to be used in its sparkling wine.

Pinot Noir produces the best wines when grown in limestone soil and relatively cool climates. Outside of France it's grown in such areas as Germany, Switzerland, Australia, New Zealand, and the United States. It emerged in California in the 1930s and has gained prominence farther north in Oregon.

Pinot Noir has been described as liquid silk. The texture is soft and velvety. Because the grape is less pigmented than other red wine grapes, the wine is lighter in color too. When it is full-bodied, it's not heavy as well. It can be ripened to high alcohol levels without the sting of tannins and acidity. Typical Pinot Noir flavors are raspberries, cherries, and smoke.

PART 6

Celebrations

From Valentine's Day to Christmas, corks can add some crafty fun to a year's worth of holidays and special events. The Folk Art Flag brings a touch of whimsy to a 4th of July BBQ, while the lovely Heart Decoration instantly warms any home. And you will find so many uses for the sweet Celebration Bunting—birthday parties, graduation celebrations, or baby or wedding showers!

TREE ORNAMENT

you will need:

* 6 corks
* Coping saw
* Sandpaper
* Power drill with 1/16" bit
* Hot glue gun
* Glitter glue
* 24 gauge craft wire
* Pliers
* Assorted beads

This rustic little tree would look great on its real-life counterpart or nestled into an evergreen wreath. You could even use it as a special gift topper, or glue one onto a wooden base to use in a little mantel scene.

1. Place 5 corks together on a table and draw cutting lines on them, as shown in the illustration.

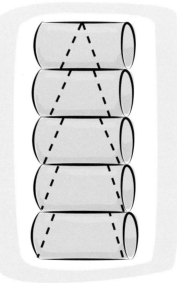

2. Cut the 5 corks on the cutting lines. Cut 1 cork in half crosswise for the trunk. Gently sand the cut edges. Brush off any dust.

3. Drill a hole through the center of the topmost cork.

4. Glue corks together, as shown.

5. Apply glitter glue to the tree. You can just do the front edges or go all the way—glitterize at will!

6. Thread wire through the hole at the top, and add beads. Make hook and attach, as shown.

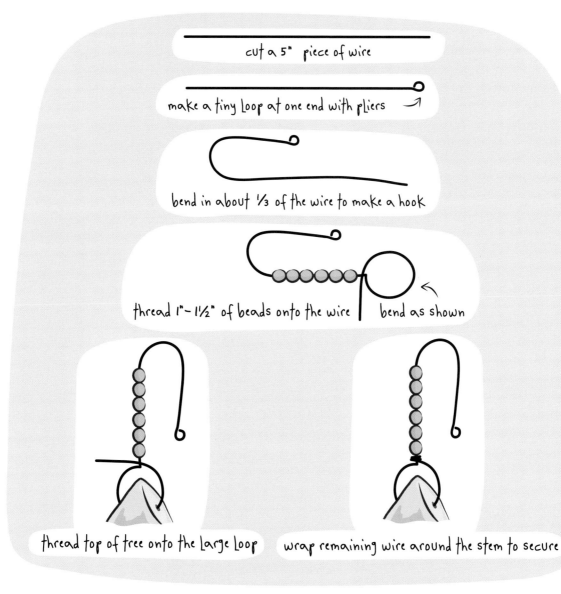

cut a 5" piece of wire

make a tiny loop at one end with pliers

bend in about ⅓ of the wire to make a hook

thread 1"–1½" of beads onto the wire   bend as shown

thread top of tree onto the large loop   wrap remaining wire around the stem to secure

Wine Profile: Riesling

If Riesling were one of the grapes in Champagne, it would undoubtedly be the world's noblest white grape, supplanting Chardonnay for the title. The physical and spiritual home of Riesling is Germany, where it's been grown for at least five hundred years and possibly as long as 2,000 years. It thrives in the coldest vine-growing climates and has found excellent homes in Alsace, Austria, Canada, and in the northern United States, in areas of New York, Washington, Oregon, and Michigan.

Riesling is rarely blended with other grapes. It doesn't need to be. It produces wines that run the gamut from bone dry and crisp to ultra-sweet and complex. Riesling is one of the few whites that have a long aging capacity. The finest will last for twenty years or more. Unlike Chardonnay, which relies on winemaker interventions for its style, Riesling relies on nature for its diversity. The winemaker really has only two decisions to make: when to pick the grapes and how long to ferment the juice.

The ripeness level of the Riesling grape at harvest drastically conditions the personality of the finished wine. In Germany, where ripeness levels vary from year to year, a system was developed to convey that ripeness level to consumers. Germany's Riesling's can de designated "Kabinett" (least ripe) all the way to "Trockenbeerenauslese" (ripest, late harvest).

HEART DECORATION

wine corks + buttons = a match made in crafty heaven

you will need:

* Hot glue gun
* 25 wine corks
* Paintbrush
* Craft paint
* 25 assorted buttons ⅝" in diameter or smaller
* Metal picture hanger

Any time is a good time of year to celebrate love, right? Show off your button collection with this sweet wall décor. This is also a good project for your not-so-interesting corks, since they are being used as a craft material rather than the aesthetic focus.

1. Glue corks together in a heart shape, as shown in the illustration.

2. Paint the heart and let it dry. You can repeat for better coverage if you like, or leave it translucent like I did. (If you are going for a more opaque finish, you could prime it first.)

3. Glue on buttons.

4. Attach the hanger to the back of the heart with glue or the small nails it may come with.

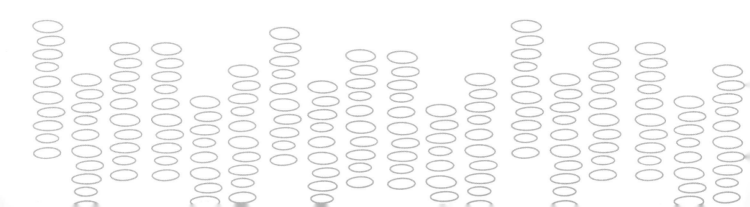

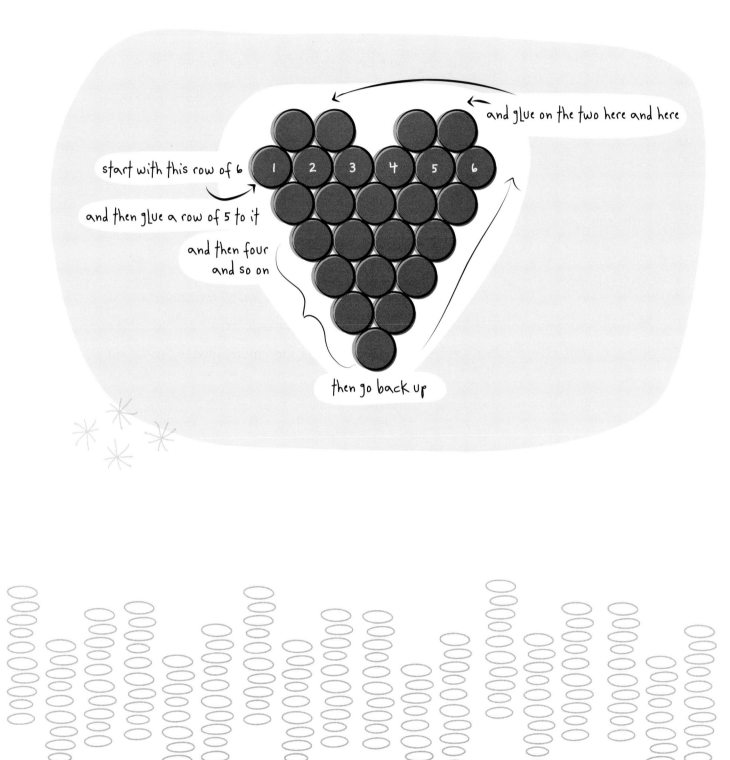

start with this row of 6

and then glue a row of 5 to it

and then four
and so on

and glue on the two here and here

then go back up

Storing Wine

Bottles with real corks should be stored on their sides to maintain contact between the cork and the wine. Without this contact, the cork may dry out, shrink, and let in air. This does not apply to bottles with synthetic corks, but make sure such bottles are still stored in cool, dark places.

SPECIAL OCCASION MEMENTO

LA GRANGE DE PLAUGIER
Marc Autran · Fils

2nd wedding anniversary

10-9-13

hang with a ribbon to make an ornament

You will need:

* Small paintbrush
* Acrylic paint
* 4" × 4" canvas
* Assorted paint pens
* Hot glue gun
* Cork from a special occasion
* Markers, pens, alphabet stamps, label makers, or printed fonts, as desired
* White cardstock
* Nail or thumbtack to hang

Instead of saving all your special wine corks in a bowl, why not memorialize an event with this lovely keepsake? You can hang several on a wall, or give one as a gift to the person you shared the moment with. These would even look great as ornaments on a tree!

1. Paint the center of the canvas, leaving a ¾" border unpainted.

2. Use paint pens to make the striped border, as shown. Add additional details if desired.

3. Glue the cork in place on the top third of the painted square.

4. In your prettiest writing, write out the date and occasion on the white cardstock. Cut out and glue under the cork. If your writing is terrible, feel free to improvise with alphabet stamps, label makers, or printed fonts from your computer, as I did.

5. Hang on a small nail or thumbtack.

teeny tiny canvases are adorable

OPTIONS!

This canvas is a perfect size to use as an ornament.
Instead of hanging with a nail, simply attach a ribbon or
string to the back.

CELEBRATION BUNTING

everybody loves bunting

You will need:

* Power drill with ³/₁₆" bit
* 14 corks
* Regular scissors
* 9 sheets of 8½" × 11" cardstock
* Assorted washi tape
* Standard hole punch
* Paintbrush
* Acrylic paint, stencils, markers, or printed fonts, as desired
* 1" wide ribbon

Who doesn't love bunting? This project is super versatile—make as instructed or change up the colors and greeting to suit the holiday or event.

1. Drill holes in the corks lengthwise. Remove crumbs from the holes.

2. Cut the cardstock into triangles, as shown in the illustration.

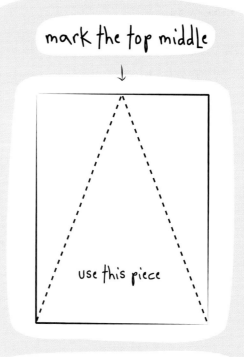

mark the top middle

use this piece

cut from the bottom corners to the top middle

3. Apply washi tape, as desired, to the bottom third of each triangle.

4. Punch 2 holes in the top of each triangle.

5. Paint on letters to spell out "celebrate." You could also use stencils, markers, or printed fonts from your computer.

6. Thread 3 corks onto the ribbon to start, and then alternate 1 triangle and 1 cork until you reach the last triangle. Finish with 3 more corks.

7. Tie knots in the ends of the ribbon to secure. Trim the ribbon so a few inches remain at the end.

OPTIONS!

If you are a quilter, you can use a dull rotary cutter blade, your quilting ruler, and a cutting mat to cut several sheets of cardstock at a time! Another option would be to use decorative scissors with a deckle, pinking, or scalloped edge. If you have all these craft supplies, use them!

Mastering Wine Lingo

When wine lovers get excited about a new wine find, they want to share the experience. The only trouble is that words are often so inadequate. Talking about wine has become intimidating, since many terms seem mysterious and pretentious. Here are some public terms that every wine lover should be familiar with.

- **Dry**—It's the opposite of sweet. When all the sugar in the grape juice has been converted to alcohol and carbon dioxide, the wine is said to be bone dry. There is a continuum, however, between really sweet and really dry. If enough residual sugar remains to give the wine a slight sweetness, the wine is off-dry.
- **Balance**—None of the wine's components is out of whack. The acid, alcohol, fruit, and tannins all work together so that one doesn't stand apart from the rest.
- **Finish**—A wine's aftertaste, or the flavor or aroma that lingers after you've swallowed the wine, is referred to as its finish. If it has one, it's considered a good thing and the longer the better. A "long finish" is a real compliment.
- **Complex**—Layers and nuances of flavor make a wine complex. A complex wine will continue to reveal itself as you sip it. This multidimensional quality is often achieved with aging. A complex wine is also said to have depth.
- **Crisp**—A wine with good acidity and no excessive sweetness is crisp. Think of an apple. The wine is relatively high in acidity, but the acidity doesn't overwhelm the other components.

In general some of the aromas you'll be able to discern from **white wines** are melon, apple, pineapple, pear, citrus, vanilla, caramel, flowers, herbs, grass, minerals, olives, and butterscotch.

Some flavors and aromas from **red wines** are berries, cedar, currants, plums, cherries, blackberries, flowers, earth, wood, smoke, chocolate, tobacco, leather, and coffee.

GIFT TAGS

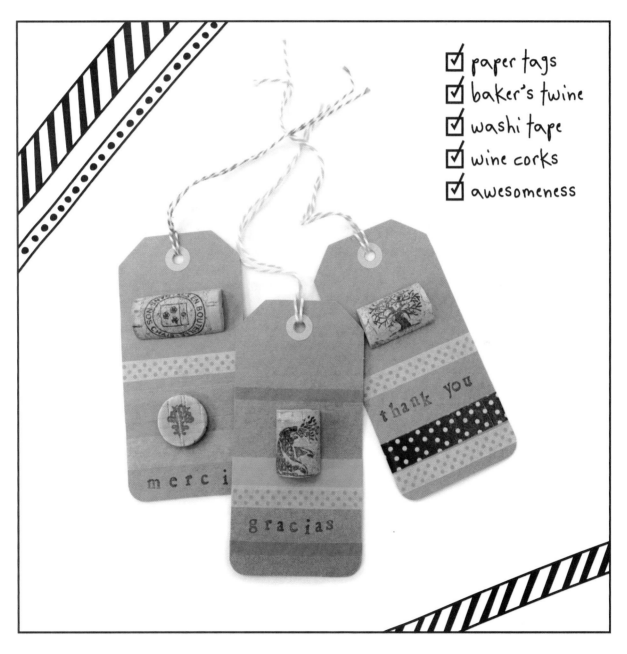

- ☑ paper tags
- ☑ baker's twine
- ☑ washi tape
- ☑ wine corks
- ☑ awesomeness

merci

gracias

thank you

You will need:

* Assorted printed wine corks
* Coping saw
* Sandpaper
* Assorted washi tape
* Paper luggage tags (available at craft stores)
* E6000 glue
* Alphabet rubber stamps with stamp pad (or fine-tip markers)
* Bakers' twine

These sweet tags are a cinch to make, plus you get to play with washi tape! Make them in bulk so you always have a cute tag to turn that bottle of wine into a thoughtful hostess gift, rather than an "I-Just-Grabbed-This-on-the-Way" kind of thing. Of course, they work great for non-wine gifts too.

1. Select the images you want to use from the printed corks and use a coping saw to cut, as desired. I cut coins from printed tops, lengthwise halves, and sections. Gently sand, wipe off dust, and set aside.

2. Apply washi tape to the top and bottom of the tags, as in the samples. Have fun mixing the different colors, patterns, and widths of tapes. Try overlapping

everyone loves washi tape

some, centering thinner tape over wider tape, or spacing them out. Leave room in the center for the corks.

3. Smear a little bit of E6000 glue onto the back of the cork and press in place on the tag. Let dry.

4. Use the alphabet stamps and ink pad to write out a greeting on the tag. I found it works best to stamp onto the paper rather than onto the washi tape. If you don't have alphabet stamps, use a fine marker and write the greeting out yourself—no big deal.

5. Cut 8"–10" length of bakers' twine and thread through the holes in the tag.

FOLK ART FLAG

you need to drink more wine
so you can make this folk art flag

you will need:

* Corks (about 145, plus a handful of extras)

* Rit powder dye in red and blue

* Hot glue gun

* Black foam board (start with a 20" × 30" piece and cut it down after the corks are glued down)

* X-ACTO knife

* Sawtooth picture hanger

This folk art–inspired Old Glory is a great first project to get started with cork dyeing. I didn't use the official number of stripes, and there are obviously no stars, but it doesn't matter—it's folk art! You're just capturing the essence and spirit of the flag.

1. Separate your corks according to what color they need to be. You can make the flag any size you like, but mine is 21" × 10.5" and these are the amounts that I used. Dye 25 corks blue (plus some extras just in case), according to the instructions in Part 1. Dye 70 red. Set aside 50 undyed corks to be the white stripes. Let dry completely.

2. Using the glue gun, start at the top row and glue corks to the foam board, as shown in the illustration, to make a flag. Glue it down so the edges of the corks hang just a little over the board. Yours will probably be different from mine because the lengths and widths of corks vary. Don't get too serious about making it perfect!

3. After all of the corks are glued down, trim the foam board from the back with an X-ACTO knife. Gently nail the picture hanger to the back.

There are lots of ways to arrange and paint the corks. Here are a few design options.

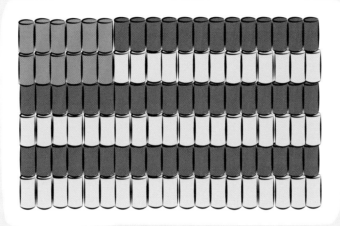

PEACE DECORATION

peace is always in season

you will need:

* Paintbrush

* Acrylic craft paint

* 1 (10") round wooden circle (available at craft stores)

* Hot glue gun

* 32 dyed wine corks (cork amounts are approximate!)

* 38 plain corks

* White school glue

* Fine glitter that matches the paint

* Sawtooth picture hanger

Peace will never go out of style. Make this decoration for any holiday or to celebrate peace every day. This project would also make a fun decoration for your tween's room, and you can let her help!

1. Paint one side of the wooden board and let dry.

2. Using the hot glue gun, glue the dyed corks on the face of the circle around the outer edge. Glue an inner row of undyed corks. You may have to move them around and space them out a little bit to get them to fit right. This is inevitable; just be patient with it.

3. Arrange undyed corks to create the stems of the peace symbol, and then glue in place.

4. Carefully paint white school glue onto the wood showing between the peace sign stems. Shake some fine glitter onto the glue and shake to cover the whole glued area. Turn the decoration over and tap to release any excess glitter. Let dry.

5. Glue hanger to the back of the decoration.

make one with a heart and one with a smiley face, too

and you've got peace, love, and happiness.

Wine Profile: Cabernet Sauvignon

The Cabernet Sauvignon (Cab, for short) has been around for fewer than six hundred years, which, in wine terms, is not long. Recent genetic studies have revealed that Cabernet Sauvignon is the offspring of the much older Cabernet Franc and Sauvignon Blanc varieties.

Cabernet Sauvignon grapes are small, black, and very tough-skinned. The thick skins make Cabernet grapes fairly resistant to disease and capable of withstanding hard autumn rains, which is a good thing because the grapes ripen late. The skins are also what give the wine its hard tannins.

Cab grapes are adaptable and can grow in almost any climate that's not too cool. They grow in most major wine-producing regions of the world. California is particularly suited to the grape, and its Cabs can command enormous prices.

Because of their often harsh tannins, young Cabernets require quite a bit of aging, first in oak barrels and later in bottles. Cabernets reward patience with velvety tannins and extraordinary complexity. Typical tasting notes on young Cabernets praise their black currant, dark berry, chocolate, and spice flavors. Older vintages are often described as having a taste of tobacco, cedar, smoke, and earth.

INDEX

Note: Page numbers in *italics* indicate projects.